Summary

The Untethered Soul

By: Michael A. Singer

Proudly Brought to you by:

Text Copyright © Readtrepreneur

All rights reserved. No part of this guide may be reproduced in any form without permission in writing from the publisher except in the case of brief quotations embodied in critical articles or reviews.

Legal & Disclaimer

The information contained in this book is not designed to replace or take the place of any form of medicine or professional medical advice. The information in this book has been provided for educational and entertainment purposes only.

The information contained in this book has been compiled from sources deemed reliable, and it is accurate to the best of the Author's knowledge; however, the Author cannot guarantee its accuracy and validity and cannot be held liable for any errors or omissions. Changes are periodically made to this book. You must consult your doctor or get professional medical advice before using any of the suggested remedies, techniques, or information in this book. Images used in this book are not the same as of that of the actual book. This is a totally separate and different entity from that of the original book titled: "The Untethered Soul: The Journey Beyond Yourself".

Upon using the information contained in this book, you agree to hold harmless the Author from and against any damages, costs, and expenses, including any legal fees potentially resulting from the application of any of the information provided by this guide. This disclaimer applies to any damages or injury caused by the use and application, whether directly or indirectly, of any advice or information presented, whether for breach of contract, tort, negligence, personal injury, criminal intent, or under any other cause of action.

You agree to accept all risks of using the information presented inside this book. You need to consult a professional medical practitioner in order to ensure you are both able and healthy enough to participate in this program.

Table of Contents

Acknowledgments viii

Introduction (The Book at a Glance) ix

FREE BONUSES xii

PART I: 14

Awakening Consciousness 14

Chapter 1. The Voice Inside Your Head 1

Chapter 2. Your Inner Roommate 4

Chapter 3. Who Are You? 7

Chapter 4. The Lucid Self 10

PART II: 13

Experiencing Energy 13

Chapter 5. Infinite Energy 14

Chapter 6. The Secrets of the Spiritual Heart 17

Chapter 7. Transcending the Tendency to Close .. 20

Part III: 23

Freeing Yourself 23

Chapter 8. Let Go Now or Fall 24

Chapter 9. Removing Your Inner Thorn 27

Chapter 10. Stealing Freedom for Your Soul 30

Chapter 11. Pain, the Price of Freedom 33

Part IV: 36

Going Beyond 36

Chapter 12. Taking Down the Walls 37

Chapter 13. Far, Far Beyond 40

Chapter 14. Letting Go of False Solidity 43

Part V: 46

Living Life 46

Chapter 15. The Path of Unconditional Happiness 47

Chapter 16. The Spiritual Path of Nonresistance .. 50

Chapter 17. Contemplating Death 53

Chapter 18. The Secret of the Middle Way 55

Chapter 19. The Loving Eyes of God 57

Conclusion..60

FREE BONUSES 63

Acknowledgments

Years ago, Linda Bean transcribed some of Michael's lectures and she encouraged him to publish a book. She worked through archived materials and soon enough, Michael began writing. Linda's dedication and commitment to this piece of work are highly appreciated.

The moment Michael started writing, Karen Entner helped him by arranging materials, coming up with content suggestions, as well as keeping the manuscript. They worked together in editing several versions until every word brought a feeling of peace to his mind, heart, and soul. Karen's heartfelt work and dedication are profoundly appreciated and the publication of Michael's book was a lifelong dream of hers.

Introduction (The Book at a Glance)

How well do you really know yourself? It's not even enough to simply know your name or the place where you live. Your self is actually bigger than what you thought you know. To understand this, you must be willing to take the step to go deeper and further within the depths of your inner being. You'll be surprised to find that life still has full of mysteries that are yet to be realized.

Freud, who is known to be the father of psychology, divided the self or psyche into three different parts: the id, ego, and superego. He considered the id to be our fundamental, animal nature. The superego acts as the method of judgment, which society has established within us. The ego is what represents us to the world outside that struggles to keep the balance between the forces of id and superego.

Most of the time, we perceive that things aren't always as simple as they appear. If we have the courage to look beyond the surface of "self," many questions start to come up that a lot of people would prefer not to ask.

In the next chapters of this book, we'll take on the journey in exploring our "self." However, we'll set our path in a different way. We won't be needing the sentiments of the well-known philosophers, or the masters in psychology. There will be no arguments, no religious views to choose, or other people's opinions to seek. Instead, we'll turn to the only source with a great firsthand knowledge on the matter. The kind of expert that has been gathering data on every moment of everyday life to provide answers to the questions. It is no other than you.

Your views and opinions on the subject are not necessary. Only your innate experience of what it's like to be you is what's important. Your knowledge is not what this book is after, but your direct experience. Failure is not an option here because your "self" is what you are all the time and in every place. Your sense of "self" just needs to be sorted out. Besides, it can become quite confusing in there.

This book consists of chapters, which simply mirrors the way you see your "self" in different points of view. Although this is an inner journey, it will rely on every detail of your life. The only thing that's needed is your willingness to sincerely look at yourself in the most natural and spontaneous way.

As you go through every page of this book, you'll find that you know more about yourself in terms of extremely complex subjects. The truth is, you already know how to find yourself, you just got distracted. Once you refocused, you'll realize that you also have the ability to free yourself. It's completely up to you. Once your inner journey is complete, you'll no longer have any reason to be confused, or to blame other people. You'll know what you need to do. You'll have a great sense of respect for who you really are.

FREE BONUSES

P.S. Is it okay if we overdeliver?

Here at Readtrepreneur Publishing, we believe in overdelivering way beyond our reader's expectations. Is it okay if we overdeliver?

Here's the deal, we're going to give you an extremely condensed PDF summary of the book which you've just read and much more…

What's the catch? We need to trust you… You see, we want to overdeliver and in order for us to do that, we've to trust our reader to keep this bonus a secret to themselves? Why? Because we don't want people to be getting our exclusive PDF summaries even without buying our books itself. Unethical, right?

Ok. Are you ready?

Firstly, remember that your book is code: **"READ120"**.

Next, visit this link: http://bit.ly/exclusivepdfs

Everything else will be self explanatory after you've visited: http://bit.ly/exclusivepdfs.

We hope you'll enjoy our free bonuses as much as we enjoyed preparing it for you!

PART I:

Awakening Consciousness

Chapter 1. The Voice Inside Your Head

There's always mental chatter happening inside the head. It never stops. It just goes on and on all day. Do you ever wonder why your mind talks endlessly?

Try taking a step back and analyze this voice. Be a little more familiar with it. Don't be too objective. Step away and watch how it talks. Notice that it grabs both parts of the conversation. You'll hear internal dialogue even when you're driving or trying to get some sleep. The problem is in the following: you tolerate it, that's why you become restless.

If you take some time to observe this voice, you'll immediately notice that not once does it ever shut up. It simply talks when left alone. It's like seeing someone who's walking and talking to his lone self.

You're the one who's both talking and listening at the same time. You even argue with this voice and you have no idea who will win the argument. It doesn't stay silent even when it's wrong.

In order to liberate yourself from the mental chatter, picture it like a vocalizing mechanism. It makes you think like there's someone else in there who's speaking to you. Don't identify what it says. If you hear it, it's clearly not you.

What's more important in terms of true growth is understanding that you're not the mind's voice. You're just the one hearing it. You can undergo many changes in life to try and find yourself, but none of these voices or personality aspects is the real you.

You'll realize that most of the things the voice tells you are meaningless. As a matter of fact, life will play out based on the forces that are beyond your control. It doesn't matter what the mind tells you about it. Life will continue to happen. Your thoughts can't influence anyone or anything, but you. The real cause of the problem is the disruption, which the mind creates about life.

Why, then, does it exist? There's actually an energy buildup inside your head that has to be unleashed, like when you're nervous or angry. Talking releases that energy.

The alternate realm that you can control is your inner world. The world outside just continues to move on with its laws. However, when the mental voice describes various external things to you, all your thoughts intermix and affect the way you experience the world. What you're really experiencing is a personal representation of the world based on you. This psychological manipulation lets you guard reality. In the world of thoughts, you can always do something to direct the experience.

Once you surpass the piece of you that's not okay, it's where real personal growth begins. Being aware that you're observing the voice while it talks is like standing at the entrance of a wonderful inner journey. If used well, it can truly lead to a genuine spiritual awakening.

Chapter 2. Your Inner Roommate

You can experience inner growth when you finally understand that you'll only feel at peace and contented when you no longer think about yourself. The "I" inside you is always facing different problems. These problems just keep on coming, one after the other.

You're never going to have a problem-free life, especially if the inner part of you has to deal with a lot of problems. Instead of asking what to do about it, try finding which part of you is troubled. If you wish to obtain peace in the midst of all your problems, you must try to figure out why a certain situation is considered a problem to you.

If you're angry, look inside you and notice which is the troubled part. If you can spot it, you're not it. It's always better to maintain unbiased recognition of the internal problem than to let yourself get lost in the outside situation. This is how you can distinguish a person who's spiritually-minded from a worldly one. A worldly person thinks that the outside world can solve his inner problems. If he can change things around him, then everything will be okay. However, to obtain real inner freedom, learn to observe your problems objectively rather than losing yourself in them. If you're angry, scared, or anxious, you won't be able to handle a situation well. You need to control your reaction first.

Rearranging things outside of you is not really a means to solve your problems. The only way is to go deeper and free that part of yourself that appears to have plenty of problems with the real world.

Your own being has a part that can separate itself from your personal melodrama. Simply be mindful of what you feel. You're the one inside who notices these things. You'll find that you're looking at someone's strong and weak aspects of personality. It's like having another person with you, like a "roommate," except that it won't even cooperate whenever you seek silence. It can easily mess everything up without giving you a notice. As soon as you realize this, you can be on your way to an actual transformation.

Once you've truly made an effort to practice being more aware and self-observant, you'll find that you can only get rid of your mental voice once you've decided that you truly want to eliminate it. As soon as you make that decision to let yourself be free of it, you're all set for the techniques and teachings. In time, you'll learn that you need to put a gap between you and your mind. You can accomplish this by setting your life paths when you're unclouded and not allowing yourself to be discouraged by the mind. Push your will to be more powerful than your habit of paying attention to that mental chatter. This is how you can reclaim your life.

Chapter 3. Who Are You?

Ramana Maharshi, a great teacher when it comes to yogic tradition, once said that to gain inner freedom, a person must sincerely and continuously ask "Who am I?" Whenever people try to ask you, "Who are you?" and you think about it, you'll realize that you've never even asked that specific question your whole life and actually meant it.

It's effortless to notice that you're different from the things you always look at. You are the subject that's examining the objects. It's easy to generalize by stating that if you're the one who's watching something, then it means that something isn't you. You know right away that the world outside isn't *you*. You're someone on the inside who's looking out, watching the world.

Still, the big question is about who you really are. Where could you possibly be if you're not on the outside world along with everything? If you pay attention, you'll know that you're still in there coming across feelings and emotions even if everything on the outside has disappeared. You're the one who's experiencing the inside sentiments and the outer world at the same time. The objects from both worlds take on one another to get your attention. Eventually, you'll understand that the stream of inner feelings and the outside world are continuously coming and going. However, it's you who remains aware of everything that passes right in front you. You're the one who experiences all of it.

Luckily, you know that you still exist even without your thoughts. For instance, when you meditate deeply, your thoughts are silent. You're just conscious that there aren't any thoughts bothering you. If you're inside going through the quietness that takes place once your thoughts break off, then your existence does not depend on thinking.

Thoughts can take a pause or get exceedingly loud. If you're aware that they exist, can't you find a way to eliminate them? Again, you're not your inner thoughts. You're just aware of them.

When the question, "Who am I?" starts be entirely important, you begin to deeply scrutinize it. You're free from the experiences and notice who's left. You're in there and you know it. You exist regardless of the thoughts.

Consciousness is total awareness. There's nothing deeper or higher than it. If it didn't exist, there will be no you. Go deeper and dwell in the place of consciousness. It's where a genuine spiritual being exist, without power and intent. When you sit far back and look outside, you'll see every thought and emotion that passes before you. You're behind every single thing you see, just watching.

Chapter 4. The Lucid Self

The lucid dream is a kind of dream where you're aware that you're in a dream. You're sensible enough to realize what you're doing, like flying. This particular distinction is precisely the difference between being aware that you're conscious in your everyday life, and not knowing that you're aware. You're no longer entirely absorbed in the circumstances surrounding you when you're aware. You just continue to be aware on the inside, experiencing the events, as well as the thoughts and feelings. You're thinking of the thought and you know it. You're lucid.

Consciousness gives you the ability to focus. Awareness is the core of consciousness and it can direct itself on specific objects. It's a natural and intuitive aspect.

With your direct experience, you can learn more about consciousness. For instance, you realize that your consciousness can be aware of numerous objects, or it can be focused on just a single object, making you forget everything else.

If you step back, you'll see that objects are always passing before you in three different levels: physical, mental, and emotional. When you're not centered, your consciousness gets attracted toward one or more of those objects and focuses on them. If it concentrates enough, your sense of awareness loses itself in the object. It's like when you're watching television, you get absorbed in the screens of mind, emotions, and outside images. All of your senses are drawn in. If you wish to re-center, just start saying "hello" inside. Relax and be aware that you can hear it being echoed in your mind.

Imagine going to a movie theater. You can see, hear, taste, smell, and touch what you're viewing. When you begin to feel the character's emotions and think their thoughts, you now have a full dimension of the experience. However, when you become bored, you start thinking about other things. Your thoughts can still occur independently of the movie. They provide an alternative place for the consciousness to focus.

When you're not being aware that you're the one watching all this, you're lost. The lost soul is the consciousness that has dropped into the place where one human's thoughts, emotions, and sensory perceptions are all synchronized. The consciousness makes the mistake of focusing on one spot too closely. When the consciousness gets sucked in, it no longer knows itself as itself. It knows itself as the objects it is experiencing. You see yourself as these objects. Your entire existing self-concept is gone and replaced by the character on screen.

When the consciousness focuses on itself, you're contemplating the sources of consciousness. This is true meditation. It is beyond the act of simple, one-pointed concentration. The focus of consciousness is turned back to the Self. You achieve a completely different state. You're now aware of who you are. That is spirituality.

PART II:

Experiencing Energy

Chapter 5. Infinite Energy

Inner energy is one of life's mysteries. We always disregard the energy within. We think, feel, and act, but we don't understand what makes it possible for all these things to happen. The truth is, every body movement, emotion, and thought that passes through your mind is a use of energy. It's not only the events that happen in the physical world that require energy, but also everything that happens inside.

For instance, if you're thinking a specific thought and another thought steps in, you'll be forced to fight that impeding thought, which requires energy. If you're feeling an emotion that you don't like, you push it aside so it won't be able to disturb you. These acts use energy.

Creating thoughts, recalling thoughts, controlling emotions, producing emotions, and directing strong inner motivation all need a massive use of energy. You can feel the inner energy when you're excited or in love, but you can also feel emotionally and mentally drained sometimes. The source of energy is drawn from inside. It's different from the outside energy source.

Your energy level can hugely shift in an instant. One moment you can feel completely tired and drained and when something excites you, you jump like you're so full of energy. This is because you have an exceptional amount of inner energy. It's something that is always accessible to you. It replenishes, recharges, and restores you.

When you don't feel this energy inside of you, it's because you're blocking it by closing your heart and mind. You hide in a dark space. This is why you feel weak when you're sad or depressed. The heart, being a center of energy, can open or close. When it's closed, energy can't flow in.

It is the spiritual energy that you're experiencing when there's love in your heart. This energy is your inheritance and it's limitless. It's doesn't get tired and old. It simply needs willingness and openness. Everybody equally has this energy.

If you want to enjoy a full life and always experience high energy, enthusiasm and love, the first thing you need to do is to decide that you want to stay open. Closing your heart is a habit you can break and control.

You tend to open or close based on your past experiences. If it's something good, you open up. If it's a negative experience, you tend to close. It happens regularly throughout our daily lives.

The more you're open, the more energy can flow inside you. Don't let anything in life be too important that you're willing to close your heart. If you close your heart, you'll only end up locking yourself inside. Don't limit yourself. Life is meant to be fun, so let go and enjoy it.

Chapter 6. The Secrets of the Spiritual Heart

The heart is a masterpiece of creation. It's a wonderful instrument made of tremendously subtle energy. When you hear or feel an instrument, such as a piano or flute, you feel it because it has touched your heart.

Not all people understand the work of the heart. It experiences certain changes. When it's open, there's love. When it closes, the love ends. When it gets hurt, we feel empty. These shifts and variations of energy that occur in the heart run your life. Nevertheless, you are not your heart. You're the *experiencer* of the heart.

The heart is really easy to understand. It is a chakra, or a center of energy that influences our day-to-day lives. It controls the flow of energy by opening and closing. If you watch it, you know what it feels like when it's open or close. The state of your heart changes all the time. You can love someone and a few days later, you no longer feel anything.

As events happen, they come in through your physical senses and affects your inner state of being. These events can bring in fear, anxiety, or love. However, it's really energy that's coming inside you when you absorb the world. When energy patterns create a disruption in your psyche, then they get blocked because you don't let them pass through you. They are kept inside and they become a problem.

Perception allows you to experience what you take in. These experiences are how you learn and grow. Your mind and heart keep on expanding as you go through one moment to the next.

It's hard to keep energy together in one place for long. This is where the mind starts to become active. When the energy can't pass through the mind, it attempts to release through the heart, creating emotional activity. When you try to fight against that release, the energy gets stored deep within the heart. In fact, everything in your life that you didn't allow to pass through you is still inside you.

When very little energy comes into your mind and heart, everything can become dark and appear negative. Over time, your heart can still get blocked, but it can also open and close often, depending on your life experiences.

It's important to understand that most of what you take in passes through you. The only ones that get blocked are those that cause problems or some feeling of excitement. Thus, you can try to push energies away because they disturb you, or you try to keep energies because you like them. Either way, you're not allowing them to pass. You're wasting energy by blocking the flow by means of resisting or clinging.

Just enjoy the gift of life. This way, you'll certainly be pushed to the depth of your being. The energy flowing in your heart will raise and inspire you. Love will feed you and strengthen you. It's the strength that will carry you through life.

Chapter 7. Transcending the Tendency to Close

Everything that's happening inside has its foundation in a hidden energy field. The movements produce our emotional and mental patterns, including our automatic reaction, inner drive and urges. This internal force field is a hidden energy flowing in specific patterns into and out of your inner being.

It's easy to see that the central energy flow is the survival instinct. There's always been the daily struggle to protect and defend oneself, but this instinct underwent evolutionary changes. The protective energies adjusted toward protecting the person mentally, instead of physically. Nowadays, we defend our self-concepts instead of our bodies. We struggle not with the outside forces, but with our own internal fears and insecurities.

Since you can't run away, you just end up hiding inside and closing down. Even when you're not aware of your energy centers, you know how to close your heart even when you're still a kid. You protect the weak part of you even though there aren't any physical danger, but because you experience emotional problems.

You'll soon realize that if you keep on protecting yourself, you'll never be free. You're locking a scared person inside your heart. You'll never grow. You allow yourself to live with very little joy and you view life as a threat.

True spiritual growth takes place when every part of you is united. Pure energy flows inside of you and your consciousness is aware of it. To achieve this state, every piece of your self should be equally open to your awareness and released.

Inner energies are strong and powerful. Your consciousness can easily concentrate on disruption. They can pull your awareness into them, but you can stop and let go. You don't have to let yourself be dragged in there. This is why it's important to be centered. Otherwise, your consciousness will follow anything that grabs its attention.

Objects come and go, while your consciousness simply watches. Your consciousness remains constant. It experiences the formation of thoughts and emotions, and it can clearly see where they are coming from without thinking about it. Your psyche is simply watching the internal energies change based on the outside and inside forces.

A simple passing thought or emotion can eventually become

the center of your life. If you don't let go, it can totally get out of control. Learn to relax and release. Be conscious enough to watch the part of you that's always trying to protect itself. Be determined to get rid of it. It will be the ultimate gift you can give yourself. You'll be free to walk in this world without having any problems. You get to enjoy and live in the present moment.

No one else can give or take your inner freedom from you, except yourself. Don't let yourself be bothered by little and meaningless things in life. Once you've learned to let go, you'll obtain peace even when you go through pain. You don't need to constantly pull yourself down. Make a decision to free yourself.

Part III:

Freeing Yourself

Chapter 8. Let Go Now or Fall

Self-exploration comes with life progression. Life has its ups and downs that can produce personal growth or personal fears. Whichever dominates depends on how we perceive change, which is something that's inevitable. It can either be frightening or exciting. Still, we must accept the fact that it is the nature of life.

What people don't realize is that fear is just another object that you can experience. You can choose to let go of it, or you can keep it and hide from it. Some people try to create a safe place for themselves so they define how they need life to be, which really makes the world frightening. When you're afraid, life throws in circumstances that challenge your attempts to be safe. You struggle with life because you resist change.

It's the fear inside us that tells us that we should determine how life should be. It prevents us from facing reality because it's beyond our control. Don't define the outside world based on your inner problems. It will surely be a terrible mess.

Protecting yourself from problems will only generate more problems. Dialogues keep going inside your head because you're trying to figure out how to stop or deal with the events that are happening. Choose not to go against life. You'll never get to fully live it if you keep on controlling it because life is constantly changing. It's possible to live without fear.

Life comes up with circumstances that push you out of your comfort zone, trying to remove what's blocking you inside. Fear is actually caused by the blockages in the energy flow. The energy can't feed your heart and your heart becomes weak, making it prone to fear.

If you want spiritual growth, you must understand that keeping things inside will only keep you trapped. After some time, you'll be wanting to free yourself. You'll realize that there are many things surrounding you that promote growth. You see it as a great opportunity to let go.

When you suddenly get pulled down into the disturbed energy, everything looks dark and depressing because you're watching from the seat of disturbance. This should remind you to let go. Otherwise, you'll only try hard to fix things. You can't clearly see what's happening. You just want the agitation to stop. Hence, you turn to your survival instincts because you want to get away from the things you don't like.

This leads to you falling into the darkness and manifesting it.

You put negative energy into your environment and it comes back to you. This is precisely how people destroy relationships, as well as their lives.

All you have to do is to let go right from the start to avoid all these mess. Open up and release the blocked energy. Let it flow up until it fuses back into your own consciousness. This will strengthen you. Always look up and get up. It is the secret of ascension. It's the secret of rising from below.

Chapter 9. Removing Your Inner Thorn

The spiritual journey is an endless transformation. You can't stay the same if you want to grow. Always embrace change. The way we find solutions to our own problems requires change. Once you accept your problems and see them as an opportunity for growth, that's the beginning of real transformation.

Imagine there's a thorn in your arm. When it is touched, you feel the pain. You only have two choices. You can either see to it that nothing touches the thorn or you can remove it from your arm. Your choices will set the course of your entire life.

If you choose the first option, you'll be working all your life to protect the thorn. Your whole life revolves around it and you might even be proud of it. You may think you have come up with a solution to your problem, but you really don't. You let this thorn run your life. It affects every decision you make every single day.

When you protect yourself from your problems, it only reflects the problem itself. You didn't solve the main cause of it; you just dedicated your whole life to staying away from it.

Notice that whenever you have a problem, instead of asking yourself how to get rid of it, you ask how you can protect yourself from feeling it. Even if you avoid situations that would make you feel or think about the problem, it will always keep on coming back. Your core problem will only expand into several problems. It affects everything around you, including your behavior.

When it comes to the human heart, we have plenty of thorns. When something touches them, it causes pain inside. Just like a person living with a thorn stuck in his arm, you end up restricting yourself. You need to make a choice. You can always choose to take out your inner thorns. It's the only way you can be totally free of them. Most importantly, don't question your capacity to get rid of the main source of the distress inside you.

In order to free yourself, you must find yourself. You're not the pain and you're not the part, which always stresses out. They have nothing to do with you. You're the one who notices these things. You can let them come up, but you can also let them go. Your inner thorns are just blocked energies from the past, which can be released. There's no reason to keep them.

Energies have been inside you your entire life. If you become aware, you'll notice that they're not you. You're simply experiencing and feeling them. If you remain centered, you'll learn to respect and appreciate your experiences, even when they seem to be difficult. When you're in the seat of consciousness, you'll experience your inner being's spirit and strength even when your heart feels weak. This is the core of the path to a spiritual life.

Chapter 10. Stealing Freedom for Your Soul

To attain true freedom, you must decide not to suffer anymore. There is no need to carry the burden brought by pain, fear, or sorrow. People only suffer because they don't know what it's like to not suffer.

What really goes on with the emotional and mental energies inside of you is that your inner vulnerability constantly brings you to a situation in which you're suffering. You're either striving to avoid or make the suffering stop, or worry about it in the next days to come.

When your suffering gets worse, that's the time you notice it and admit that you have a problem. It creates an impact on your behavior and your inner voice gets anxious. You always think about yourself because you're not okay inside. You're always trying to make yourself feel better. You go around trying to change things around you so you can please yourself. You must understand and accept that your psyche is not okay, but it can be all right. When fear is present, that's your psyche trying to talk to you.

Your psyche becomes afraid when you mistreat it. You're providing it with certain responsibilities that are impossible to understand. For instance, you keep on thinking about trying to please everyone all the time. The mind has to make sure everything goes your way. You're giving it an impossible task. It's like forcing your body to lift huge trees.

When you worry about yourself, you suffer. Your thoughts are directed towards what's troubling you at the moment. Your mind tells you that there's something outside that needs to change to solve your inner problems. However, it's not a good advice. Because your mind is disturbed by fears, it can misguide you.

Outside situations only try to solve the problem, not to cause inner problems. For instance, if you feel lonely, being in a relationship is your effort to solve your problem. You're trying to find out if that relationship will calm your internal disturbance. Still, it's not the solution to the source of your problem.

On the other hand, to achieve success in terms of your psyche, you shouldn't think about it or dedicate your life to it. Imagine what it's like without those upsetting thoughts. You can truly live and experience life, instead of trying to fix yourself.

You can live a life without the fear of your "self". All you have to do is to stop forcing the mind to fix your own problems. It cannot manipulate everything around you. If it's trying to talk to you, ignore it. Once you're okay with everything, then everything will be okay.

Relax and be quiet. You're not the thinking mind. You're simply aware of it. You're the consciousness behind it that's aware of the thoughts. You watch the mind think. This way, you're actually liberating yourself.

Chapter 11. Pain, the Price of Freedom

Change isn't always comfortable. It challenges what we know and questions our needs. It is often recognized as a heartbreaking experience. Coming to peace with pain is necessary for personal transformation and spiritual growth. You must be able to face your inner disturbances. You'll then realize that pain is seated in the core of your heart, which is why you spend your life trying to avoid it.

Pain can influence everything you do. Unlike physical pain, inner pain always exists. It only hides underneath your thoughts and emotions. You can really feel it when your heart goes into confusion. If you really want to grow, you must learn to deal with pain.

Any behavior pattern based on the prevention of pain turns into a doorway to pain itself. The feelings you experience will work their way back to the motive behind your actions. For instance, if you're scared of being rejected and you approach a person, when that person says something wrong, you'll feel the pain of rejection.

Pain comes from the heart. This is the reason why you feel a lot of agitation throughout the day. The pain that is not processed creates more layers of sensitivities every time you try to avoid it. For example, in order to keep your friendship with others, everything you do must be acceptable to them. You think about several ways to present yourself. You've gone layers and layers and further away from the core pain. You end up becoming so sensitive that everything you do affects your heart and causes pain.

You need to get some perspective to distance yourself from this. Walk outside or stare at the night sky. There are billions of stars in the galaxy and you're just standing on a ball of dirt, spinning around one of those stars. From that point of view, would you really care what other people think of you?

You can choose to leave the pain inside and keep struggling with the outside, or you can get rid of the inner pain. You can only be free if you don't let pain run your life. Think of the inner pain as a temporary shift in the flow of your energy. You don't have to be afraid of the experience. You can't spend your life avoiding things that are not even happening. Pain can just be a feeling that you can handle. Whatever happens, you're okay with it. It can't touch you unless you touch it.

Don't let pain shape you, your thoughts, reactions, and preferences. You must learn to go beyond your habit of avoiding pain. Many things happen every day that cause an inner disturbance. Stop fighting your feelings. Pain is simply an energy that you must allow to pass through.

There are freedom and joy on the other side of pain. You must be willing to accept pain to pass through to the other side. Once you feel comfortable with it, there's no reason to be scared of yourself. There's nothing that the world can do to hurt you. You're free. Pain is the price of freedom.

Part IV:

Going Beyond

Chapter 12. Taking Down the Walls

As you continue to grow, your inner "self" becomes a lot quieter. You'll realize that you've been in there this whole time. It's just that you've been overwhelmed by this flood of thoughts and emotions. You'll start to think that it's actually possible to surpass all these disruptions. Since you're completely separated from the things you're watching, there's a way to be free from the hold that your psyche has over your awareness.

Enlightenment is the inner breakthrough to complete freedom. However, the term itself is often misunderstood since it is based on our limited understanding and personal experiences.

Take this story as an example. Imagine you're in a beautiful open place with great light. You immediately decided that you wanted to live there. You bought it and started to build your dream house. It even has separate quarters so your housekeeper could leave you alone. When it was finished, you loved every part of it because you put your heart and soul into every aspect of the house.

Over time, you started spending more time indoors until you

became used to living safely within the confines of the house. Inside the house, everything was predictable, familiar, and within your control. Meanwhile, the outside world was uncertain, unknown, and out of your control.

You got so used to never turn off the lights, but eventually they started burning so you had to use a few candles. It was hard for you because you're a person who loves light. Still, your fears about leaving the safety of your house are much stronger. The darkness eventually harmed your physical and mental health. What was once a beautiful place started to fade from your mind.

Soon, you became lonely. You forgot why you're so scared. You're just aware of being so uncomfortable. You even stopped doing the things you love. You were falling into the darkness.

All of a sudden, your housekeeper called you down to the storage cellar. You were surprised to see it fully radiant because of all these emergency flashlights stored in there. It became a turning point in your life.

You began creating beauty, light, and happiness within your house. You worked together to keep the light shining brightly. Love began to shine in both of your hearts. You even married each other and promised to bring light and love into your home. It was heaven.

One day, you came across a book in your library that talked about the natural light that exists outside. You felt so confused because you've been living for so long inside that dark house that you don't know how to go outside.

That house is all your thoughts, emotions, past experiences, and dreams. You pulled and knit them all together into a conceptual world in which you live. This mental structure blocks you from whatever natural light is on the outside.

Don't be afraid to go past these walls. Don't hide in the darkness. You can get out by letting life take down your walls. When your walls crumble down and consciousness is released, flourishing in its own brilliance, that is true enlightenment.

Chapter 13. Far, Far Beyond

Going beyond simply means going past where you are. You don't just stay in your present situation. There are no boundaries or limitations when you always go beyond yourself. Beyond is immeasurable in all ways. The truth is, everything is limitless. Things only appear to be limited because your consciousness runs into mental boundaries.

You must keep going past the limits you put on things so you can go beyond. This means changing something within yourself. Right now, your logical mind creates an alternative reality of limited thoughts that remain fixed in your head. This is because you want to try to control things. You end up constantly struggling to fit certain pieces together to make a world that fits your model of reality. If things don't fit, you label them as bad or wrong.

When something happens that challenges your perception of things, you get frustrated and you fight. If you wish to surpass it, you must not believe in it. Try understanding why you built a mental model in the first place and see what happens when it doesn't work. You actually end up struggling to keep your world from collapsing.

Your world doesn't need to fall apart for you to realize what you're doing. If you want to see why you do certain things, don't do them. For instance, if you want to know the reason you're smoking, then stop smoking. See what happens when you don't do the things that make you comfortable. You always try to stay within your comfort zone. Otherwise, you feel uncomfortable and your mind tells you to fix things. Everything you do keeps you restricted.

You can choose to remain in your comfort zone or you can work on your freedom. Imagine what it's like to be like a tiger inside a cage. It can be extremely frightening. Your comfort zone creates a similar cage. It doesn't limit your body; it limits the area of your consciousness.

Fear makes you want to stay inside this cage. You're afraid because what's beyond is unknown to you. You want to feel safe that's why you don't want to get out. You have fallen in love with your cage.

When you are spiritually awake, you'll realize that you are locked up in a cage. You're always hitting the walls of your comfort zone. You start to see that you can't freely express yourself because you're too self-conscious. Since you've set some limits on yourself, once you approach your limits, you start to feel anxious and insecure.

The moment you're willing to go beyond and face reality without mental boundaries, your soul becomes free and infinite. You go on your day with an inspired and peaceful heart. Spirituality is the commitment to go beyond, no matter what it takes.

Chapter 14. Letting Go of False Solidity

The psyche is a complex place with conflicting forces that keeps on changing due to external and internal events. In just a short amount of time, various fears, needs, and desires build up and we end up struggling to hold it all together. We spend most of our time trying to control and keep everything in order.

When you struggle, you suffer. Trying to hold everything together is already a form of suffering, especially when things start to fall apart. Your psyche becomes troubled and you fight to keep your innermost world together. Nevertheless, the truth is, there's nothing solid in there in which you can cling to.

As you go deeper into yourself, you'll realize that your consciousness is always there. It's a dynamic field of awareness that can broadly expand or narrowly focus. Your sense of self is then determined by where you are directing your consciousness.

When you become focused on a particular object, it moves slowly. The force of consciousness ends up holding the objects steady just by focusing on it. This act creates clinging.

When you cling to a specific thought or emotions, it can remain in one place long enough to block the psyche.

The objects you cling to are used to create a sense of orientation and security in the middle of the nonstop inner change. You make a structure of clear solidity and you end up building your entire self around it. However, you'll never find yourself in what you have built to define yourself. You just allowed yourself to become lost.

Your sense of stability creates a false sense of security. As a result, when you can't anticipate the behavior of the people around you, it disturbs you.

People put facades out there. All of us are always clinging and building. We try to create someone and when that someone is what others want and need, you can be quite popular and successful. The society has a lot to say about everything. Think about it. When people behave based on your expectations, you treat them nicely, but when they don't, you either pull back from them or get angry.

What people don't know is that the clinging can stop. You don't have to hold on to your experiences in order to build yourself. You just need to be brave enough to let go and face your fears. Let the moments come and go. It's the only way you can stop struggling and attain peace. When you don't take part in this struggle, you can live spiritually.

You don't have to live like everybody else. You can be completely free to experience life. You can be filled with light and your inner force will guide you from the inside. You'll be at peace. When you're at peace with your true being, there's no room for false solidity.

Part V:

Living Life

Chapter 15. The Path of Unconditional Happiness

Life itself is the highest path to spirituality. Everything becomes a liberating experience when you know how to live your everyday life. To do this, you only have to make one choice. You need to decide if you want to be happy or not. If you choose to be happy, then your life path becomes absolutely clear.

People usually don't give themselves a choice because they think it's beyond their control. Their number of preferences gets in the way. If you really want to be happy, say it without any limitations to it. You must want it regardless of what happens in life. There shouldn't be any ands, buts, or ifs. You'll only give a limit to your happiness if you create a condition. Your choice must be unconditional. You must really mean it when you say that you want to be happy. Unconditional happiness is the biggest means there is. You'll not only be happy, but you'll also be enlightened.

The moment you decide to be happy, challenges will become inevitable. Your commitment will be put to the test, which ultimately promotes spiritual growth. It's really not easy to be happy when everything isn't going well.

The purpose of life is to enjoy and learn from your experiences. You're not born to suffer. Being miserable doesn't help anybody. You came into this world and you're going to die. What you do during your time in between is your choice. It's not the events that determine whether you're going to be happy or not. You get to choose that for yourself.

Let go of the part of you that constantly creates melodrama. The only sensible thing to do is to enjoy life's experiences. There's nothing you can gain out of pain and suffering, so don't let the things you can't control bother you.

Choosing to enjoy life is a spiritual teacher itself. Once you commit to unconditional happiness, you'll learn more about yourself, about others, and about life. You'll learn more about your heart and mind. Always stay open. It also helps to use affirmations. If you commit yourself to being happy, nothing would be able to stop you.

The key is to understand your inner energies. If you look deep within yourself, you'll find that your heart feels open when you're happy and energy keeps flowing inside. Don't try to close your heart whenever you feel sad. You have that choice to not give up your happiness.

If you stay open, positive energy will surely fill your heart. Spiritual practices bear fruit when you learn to stay open. You'll never know how many great things you can find. It's possible to reach the state of bliss and freedom. The joy you feel can become overpowering, and it's such a beautiful path to take.

Chapter 16. The Spiritual Path of Nonresistance

Your spiritual work must lead towards learning to live a life without fears, problems, stress, or melodrama. Stress only happens when you resist the changes in life's events. When you simply live in the present, you won't create any resistance. You're just witnessing and experiencing life as it happens.

You must first understand why you try so hard to defy life. If you look within yourself, you'll find that it's actually you who has this certain kind of power. It's called willpower.

Will is a force that springs from your being. It's what makes your body move. You use the same will to hold on to your thoughts when you want to focus on them. It's also what you use when you try to make things happen, or when you prevent something from happening. You have the power to influence things.

Trying to resist the things that happened doesn't change the fact that they still happened. What you're really trying to resist is the experience passing through you and it will only affect you inside.

In time, you'll realize that this resistance is just a waste of energy. You're basically using your willpower to resist the outcomes from the past or thoughts about the future. Anything you do will just cause more disturbance. The energy that needs to be released has no place to go. It gets stuck in your psyche and severely affects you.

Because we tend to struggle with past energies, we become unprepared to face the present events. Over time, we become so blocked that we get stressed-out or completely burned-out.

The personal events that happen in our lives leave marks on our hearts and minds. They become the foundation for our will to either cling or resist. Because of these, you resist the current events, which creates inner struggle and tension. You think these past events have meaning, but the truth is, they just ruin your life.

You need to use life and be very conscious. You need to cautiously watch the mental voice as it tries to speak to you. It will give you advice and tell you to resist the world, but don't listen to it. Let your spiritual path become the willingness to allow whatever happens pass through you. Start by dealing with every situation with acceptance. Accept that events are not personal problems, they're just events taking place in this world.

Take a pause and think about what you're capable of achieving if you don't let your inner struggles restrain you. The world eventually becomes a different place. You could actually do anything. You could transform your life if you let your heart and mind become open and wide enough to embrace reality. You'll feel more love, peace, and contentment.

Chapter 17. Contemplating Death

It is indeed a great contradiction that death turns out to be one of life's best teachers. Death teaches you things that nothing else and no else can teach you. However, the real question is, are you going to wait that long and let death become your teacher?

A wise individual understands that at any time or place, his life can be taken away from him. He embraces the fact that death is unpredictable and inevitable.

Death doesn't have to be the one things that challenge you to live at your highest level. You don't have to wait until everything is gone before you learn to dig down deep within yourself to reach your highest potential. The moment you realize this, it's actually the consciousness you need to create deep and meaningful relationships.

People usually take things for granted because they think that other people would still be there when they wake up the next day. But what if they aren't? Imagine what it would be like to live like every person you care about could be taken away at any moment. Your life will surely be different.

Death is not a morbid thought. In fact, it's a wonderful idea that you can think about. Surely, if you know that you could be taking your last breath at any moment, then you wouldn't waste your time and energy focusing on things that don't really matter. With this truth in mind, you should be brave enough to constantly reflect on how you're living your life. People who have experienced true awakening fully live their lives without making any compromises.

You don't have to be afraid to talk about death. Instead, allow this knowledge to help you or guide you on how to live every moment of your life, because every single one of them matters. Everything can be a million times more meaningful.

Death can change everything in an instant. When you embrace this truth, you don't really have to change your life, just the way you live it. It's not about what you're doing, it's how much of you is doing it.

Start using every day to say what you need to say and do what you need to do. Be fully present without fearing what could happen next. Don't fear death. Instead, allow it to free you. Allow it to encourage you to live your life to the fullest. Live as if you're facing death all the time. Don't be afraid of life. Growth from experience is the only thing you can get from it. The willingness to live is what gives life meaning. Death makes life precious.

Chapter 18. The Secret of the Middle Way

The path to spiritual life isn't complete without addressing one of the deepest of all spiritual teachings, the *Tao te Ching*. "The Tao" means "the Way." It is so delicate that people only talk around its edges, but never truly touch it. It is a treatise in which the very basis for the principles of all of life is laid down.

Unfortunately, many spiritual teachings hide the center of truth with mystical words. Nevertheless, with Tao, it's simple. People who have truly learned the secrets of life understand these truths without reading anything. If you want to understand Tao, you must take it slow and keep it simple. Otherwise, you may miss it even when it's already right in front of you.

Everything has two extremes and the Tao is in the middle. It's the place where there is the balance. There's no energy pushing it in either direction. Everything remains in peaceful harmony.

You have to realize that everything has its yin and yang and its own balance point. It's the order of all these balance points, woven together, that forms the Tao. This overall balance maintains its equilibrium as it moves through time and space. Energies are pulled to the center so that it wouldn't be wasted going sideways. Staying centered gets something done.

In every aspect of life, if you're in balance, your body stays healthy. Being in extremes also teaches you many things. When you analyze them, it's easy to see the results of imbalanced behavior patterns.

The more extreme you are, the less forward movement there is. You only end up getting stuck. Simply let the extremes go. You'll see that all the energy that had been wasted will be easily accessible to you. You'll become much clearer and the experience of being present in each moment will become a natural state for you. Events that take place in life will no longer appear confusing or overwhelming.

Almost everyone has a point at which they get out of balance. However, whoever stays present with the fixture of purpose always ends up coming out on top.

When you move in the Tao, life becomes totally simple. Life unfolds while you feel for the center. All things move quietly through that center balance. The Tao is there in everything. It is completely at peace. You can't touch it, but you can be at one with it.

Chapter 19. The Loving Eyes of God

We all have different teachings, concepts, and views about God, but how can anyone really know anything about Him? Fortunately, there's a direct connection to the Divine deep within us. There's a part of our being that's beyond the personal self and you can consciously choose to identify with that part. It's where a natural transformation starts to take place inside of you. You can know the nature of God by looking into the mirror of your changed "self". This is a direct experience.

Over time, you'll start to stray away from the feelings of tension and anxiety. Although the cloud of lower vibrations may still be there, you stop thinking they're you or that there's anything you have to do about them. Your Spirit drifts upward as you learn to let go of them. You know it because you experience it.

Your being draws further back inside yourself. You start to feel more spaciousness inside. You don't feel fear, anger, or resentment towards other people. You don't close your heart. You feel like you're going somewhere and you're actually going into your spiritual being. You identify more with the flow of pure energy.

Now you walk around feeling love for no reason. The Spirit always feels good, open and light. Because of this, you center more and more on the spiritual part of your being. As you willingly release the physical, mental and emotional aspects of your being, the Spirit becomes your state. Everything becomes more beautiful.

Still, how can you really know God or anything that's beyond you? You know because the people who have gone beyond came back and told you that the Spirit you're experiencing is the gateway to God. They have felt great love and light waking up inside them and their sense of Self-merging with it. Just like what's stated in the Gospel of John, that one can merge into God. This is how you know Him. You become one with Him.

Imagine what would happen if you begin to feel great love towards every creature. There's no judgment. There's only loving, respecting and appreciating.

Knowing God must come from actual experience. It's what happens when you meditate, or let go of your lower "self". You drift into Spirit and transformations happen inside of you. You just need to notice them. You'll get a glimpse of what it must be like to sit in that Divine State.

There's no impurity. Everything is just beautiful. You embrace other people's whole being. That's how it is through the eyes of love. If God is love, the eyes are filled with endless love and compassion. And indeed, you have a loving God.

Conclusion

Life can be really simple. All you have to do is just to know your inner "self". There's truly more to everything than we thought we already know. It's such a great way to live knowing that there's more to learn when you've uncovered one of life's greatest mysteries.

No matter what you say or do, or where you go, there is always you. You are always conscious of the things passing through your physical senses. It's just that sometimes, you get too distracted with the opposing voices going on inside your head. You don't have to listen to those voices. You just need to let it go.

Your life depends on you, not on the things around you. The outside world is full of chaos that once you let it affect you, you can easily fall into the trap of darkness. Keep your heart open and don't lock yourself inside whenever things don't go your way. The ability to live freely is within you. Positive energies are always available inside of you, if only you'll learn how to release the negative thoughts and emotions that's usually dragging you down.

If you want to grow, don't let fear take control over you. It only leads to more pain and suffering. If you surrender to fear, you'll end up locking yourself in a cage. You're depriving yourself of the great things that the world can still offer you. Take the steps toward the other side of fear. There you'll find freedom, joy, and love.

Learn to accept that life will continue to unfold no matter what you do and the events won't always be what you expect them to be. You can't control everything, but don't let it stop you from being happy. Instead, when bad things happen, you simply experience it and learn from it. You don't have to cling to it. Let it all go and keep moving forward.

Life isn't about trying to please everyone. Your happiness doesn't depend on anyone. The outside world won't be able to solve the real problem that's inside of you. Be conscious enough not to torture your mind thinking about how you should live your life to be accepted by others. You can stop listening to your thoughts and let all the melodrama simply slip through your mind. Be who you really are.

While pain can be uncomfortable, you can see it as a way to grow spiritually. Go beyond your comfort zone. Experience life. It's all about making a choice between being happy and being miserable. Surely, you don't want to pick the latter. Nothing is worth being miserable over.

CONCLUSION

Don't waste your precious time and energy doing things that stop you from freely expressing yourself. You don't need to hide in the dark. Follow your heart and experience life. It is God's greatest gift to you because God is love. Walk towards the path of light and happiness. Live with absolute freedom and love. You can always choose to live a meaningful and beautiful life.

FREE BONUSES

P.S. Is it okay if we overdeliver?

Here at Readtrepreneur Publishing, we believe in overdelivering way beyond our reader's expectations. Is it okay if we overdeliver?

Here's the deal, we're going to give you an extremely condensed PDF summary of the book which you've just read and much more…

What's the catch? We need to trust you… You see, we want to overdeliver and in order for us to do that, we've to trust our reader to keep this bonus a secret to themselves? Why? Because we don't want people to be getting our exclusive PDF summaries even without buying our books itself. Unethical, right?

Ok. Are you ready?

Firstly, remember that your book is code: **"READ120"**.

Next, visit this link: **http://bit.ly/exclusivepdfs**

Everything else will be self explanatory after you've visited: <http://bit.ly/exclusivepdfs>.

We hope you'll enjoy our free bonuses as much as we enjoyed preparing it for you!

CPSIA information can be obtained
at www.ICGtesting.com
Printed in the USA
BVHW070840231019
561861BV00001B/97/P